Blue Thirst

Lawrence Durrell

CAPRA PRESS ❧ 1975 ❧ SANTA BARBARA

With special thanks to Cynthia Sears.

ISBN 0-88496-017-X (pa.)
ISBN 0-88496-018-8 (hb.)

CAPRA PRESS
631 State Street
Santa Barbara, California 93101

My first impulse when I received these two transcripts of impromptu lectures I gave in California, was the normal one, namely to sit down and rewrite them, to give the prose some shape. But then, on reflecting, it seemed to me that it would be better to leave them just the way they were, with all the hesitations and fumblings and false starts. They seemed more actual that way; I thought that if I tidied them up I might take all the life out of them. The result is that whatever small changes I have made have been only in the interests of intelligibility; there were defective patches in the transcript, and sometimes in the typing. These I touched up lightly, but careful to keep the colloquial tone, and the hesitations which are inevitable in impromptu lecturing.

The first lecture was given in the marvelous Beckmann Auditorium at Caltech in Pasadena under the general title "A Poet In The Mediterranean." The second was perpetrated at Claremont College, Pomona. My grateful acknowledgements go to both institutions for permission to reprint.

Lawrence Durrell
Paris, 1975

Blue Thirst

Blue Thirst

An invitation to reminisce is always rather terrifying. One inevitably thinks of those old after-dinner speakers, rosy with fatuity, who somehow can't break off. So when I received an invitation to reminisce I was a little bit tormented by doubts because I remembered also another cautionary tale—the curate, the shy curate in Leacock, a wonderful short story, where he found that every time he said, "Well, I think I ought to. . . ," they said "Won't you have another cup of tea?" And he was too weak to leave. He sank back into his chair finally lingered until dinner time and they said "Do you really have to go home? We could easily give you dinner." And he was too weak, he stayed for dinner. Finally, they had to make—they were naturally furious—they had to make up a bed in the spare room. And he stayed there for weeks in a strange delirium, sometimes rising up from his pillow he would cry, "I really think I must. . ." and then sink back hopelessly with a cracked laugh. Finally as you may remember, the angels came for him. I didn't want them to come for me.

Nevertheless I did feel that perhaps there might be some point in trying to recollect and perhaps recreate a little bit of a Greece which is not finished now and gone for good, but which has changed very much and doesn't resemble the Greece that I knew at the age of 21 when I was a young aggressive poet. It was in Greece that I first hit the Mediterranean proper. And thinking it over I thought I might perhaps accept and have a try at repainting this not forgotten but not so terribly distant Greece in time.

The land I went to then was not the popular one it is today—Italy was the in thing. Everybody great had given a *cachet* to Italy, from the Romantic poet onwards. Byron was the only person who went to Greece, but he did it for a special reason. But the Greece I met presented enormous practical day-to-day problems.

It was the era before DDT. I have to remind you how recently the medicaments which make Mediterranean travel easy and pleasant are—DDT was discovered only during the last war. Greece was one large flea before then. One enormous hairy gnashing flea. And several kinds of bedbug as well, mostly elephant-size. And walking across it in the heat, the primitiveness of the country was really intimidating. It was in some ways almost as primitive as Africa. If it hadn't been so beautiful and washed always by this marvelous blue sea, it would have really daunted even me, and I was tough and in very good health. But our Greece we learnt the hard way and we learnt it without penicillin and any of the amenities which are available now. The big miracle drugs, for example, that breakthrough was also at the end of the war: The sulphanilamides—a whole range of science that wasn't available to us in 1934. One was deep in the Middle Ages in a remote Greek village. The actual medical arrangements were in the hands of a few kind pharmacists and women called "good women" who were kind of medieval bone-setters and also masseurs with a marvelous sense of anatomy. They really did perform wonders. I have seen miracles performed with them—and also nobody quite knows how they got their special knowledge because they have enough sense to leave a tubercular bone alone. But they were great manipulators of limbs and even today they are still there and perform astonishing cures. They are also specialists in herbal cures. In those days I elected to live in a Greek village the life of a fisherman. The house that I took is on the north end of the island of Corfu which is extremely beautiful and which I found by accident. Later on it was literally a question of putting a pin in a map and saying to my mother "You've got to stop spending money and start economizing." In those days Greece was unbelievably cheap and she managed to live very satisfactorily with her family in a large house. My brother has described all this inimitably and powerfully in a wonderful book. And I think here I should say that I feel extremely pleased that I am responsible in part for two of the best books about modern Greece. One is Henry Miller's book which is partly due to the fact that I took him there and he fell in love with it and wrote probably his best book there. And then my brother's own book is marvelous because he literally wasn't aware that there was an ancient Greece. It was extraordinary how he felt his way back into his 12-year-old skin to write it. Naturally in it his older brother figures as a sort of horrible Faustian figure. I was 22 and writing the *Black Book* at that time. And he paid off all his youthful grudges in the book, quite rightly. The book is really a masterpiece as a picture of Corfu simply because there is not a single classical reference in it. The seduction—you smile, but in fact it is perfectly true—the seduction about Greece is such that one tends towards purple prose all the time and it's very difficult to see a Greek landscape or a Greek village without thinking of Aphrodite or a modern Greek situation which doesn't immediately echo something Homeric. So naturally, if you have an Aphrodite in your pocket you tend to plaster it into your prose and consequently it's just not as good as somebody treating Greece as if it was entirely new, pristine, fresh and born yesterday—a new-laid egg. And Miller deliberately ignored the classical stuff he knew and my brother didn't know any. So between them they produced wonderful books of which I am rather proud because I took both of them there.

It's funny, I've often thought, and philosophers have frequently said, that one remembers the hard beds better than the soft ones. And those winters in Greece were extraordinarily hard, particularly living in unheated houses with no chimneys and no wood in the north of this island. The rainfall in Corfu is almost tropical in density—that is why it is so green. But sometimes one heard it for weeks on end—that and the sea pounding on the rocks below the house we lived in.

My brother very skillfully gave the impression that I lived with the family, but that wouldn't have been possible. You don't know how awful they are. I always lived apart from them but I used to visit them at Christmas just to observe them. And make a few notes. But I always lived with my wife alone on the north point of the island in a very lonely and rather beautiful house. And as I say, our life was one of the utmost primitiveness—in terms of food I don't remember what it was possible to find—apart from the few fish we caught—to eat, because the roads were washed out in the winter and apart from a few tins of macaroni I think we literally had nothing. Occasionally they killed a lamb, Greek lamb isn't bad, it's—well, I suppose it was horrible, our diet, but when you're young and in good health it didn't seem to matter very much.

There were other factors about ordinary living which I mustn't forget to mention, just to draw the picture of this rather primitive way of life. In this hot country, indeed in most of the Mediterranean at this time there was no refrigeration; just a few ice factories where one bought blocks of ice and crammed them into wooden ice boxes. In Corfu there was no butter and the milk was goat's milk; the beef was non existent, there was only lamb for people with small incomes but good lamb and sometimes pork. Chickens were thin and scrawny.

The best refrigerator I know is a deep well; and for most of my island life we lowered our bottles and tinned butter down the well in a basket with a long length of line. Or shoved it into a sea cave. Sometimes it was so hot that we carried our dinner table out into the bay and set it down in the water. It was cool enough if you sat with water up to your waist while you dined. The water was so still and clear that the candles hardly moved on such summer nights. And the bronze moon was huge.

Our heating system was mostly charcoal, which meant twenty minutes to boil a kettle for a cup of tea with much puffing and blowing. Primus stoves were very expensive and had a tendency to explode. As for light we used paraffin with its peculiar smell and though the Aladdin lamp had been invented it was expensive and was hard to obtain mantles.

The roads were washed out in winter and the little local bus service was *caïques* in summer; but when the sea was high they couldn't go. Most of you now have been to Greece or have seen enough of Greece in pictures to know those little island boats which ferry the melons and the fruit and vegetables back and forward. Well, they're also passenger buses, and in summer we had a daily waterbus to town which took two hours flat and the same back in the evening which took two and a half hours flat according to what the wind and weather was like. This fragile line of communication was completely washed out in the winter and we were left alone on this extraordinary hillside. I started at once to try and learn Greek, which is a very difficult language. I'd only done two years of classical Greek and it really wasn't enough. I hadn't been interested until I got there. But there were things which struck me very forcibly and touched me very much. Mainly that when I was starting on doing Demotic Greek with the local schoolmaster, I found that in almost any Greek sentence about 3 out of 5 words—no that's an exaggeration—let's say 3 out of 7 words came out of Aristotle or Homer. And it was a perfectly astonishing realization to me that Greece hadn't aged—the language that Greece used—hadn't aged as much as our own English because we started with the old Attic grammar and while a lot of the tenses had changed, and naturally a lot of vocabulary had changed and so on, the actual structure of the language as such is quite visibly there, still. And I don't think you could begin to teach English out of Chaucer, which would be roughly the comparison to today. And then Homer became more actual to me in this context, and I started brushing up the little ancient Greek I knew, and a whole winter, my first whole winter passed in that way, studying, teeth chattering with cold. There was no chimney in the house and finally my landlord put logs in an ordinary room there and burnt them so that the room filled with smoke and the smoke went out steadily through the ceiling. It was more Homeric than Homer. We roasted lambs on the spit and mopped up the blood. And drank *retzina*, the resined wine of Greece.

But there were also other fascinating things. When I started to learn Greek it was the popular tongue I studied, the so-called Demotic. But I rapidly realized that there were two distinct Greek languages—one for the newspapers and one for the hearth. The popular one had evolved itself comfortably by peasant use, and a much simplified syntactical approach. But this was considered too vulgar to write down, and a highly purified sort of Greek had been evolved for the newspapers, thus causing a great and unnecessary problem for schools and parents. Can you imagine talking the way you do in ordinary life and yet being forced to read Elizabethan prose every time you opened the *Los Angeles Times*, with a classier and more classical vocabulary? This has been a real plague for the Greek poets and only now has the battle been won for Demotic Greek thanks to half a century of taming and civilizing this language for the uses of poetry. But at the turn of the century when someone suggested turning the Bible into Modern Demotic Greek there were street battles and deaths. Only a highly educated classics scholar could read the Bible then, and the priests didn't want to let the peasants know the meaning of what they read or chanted. This battle was carried on—the battle of the two languages—and when I was there there were even two different words for 'wine' and 'bread.' Well by great luck an enlightened Minister of Education—whom you will know under the name of Kazanzakis, author of *Zorba The Greek*— gave permission for the Greek classics to be turned into modern Greek for the schools; and so the children of Greece came at last into the heritage of their native literature, and could read Homer and Sophocles in a good crib, as we would call it in England. Well, the two kids of my landlord were then going to the village school and were being taught Homer in a pretty story-book version. They came back at dusk usually, but one night I heard the whole family talking and laughing until the late hours. It was strange because they usually were in bed by the time darkness fell in order to save fuel. I felt that something special must have happened. The next morning the landlord came to me and said "Oh gosh, I've got the most wonderful story these kids are reading. I wish I could explain it to you, but your Greek isn't good enough. It's apparently by a man called Homeros. What a pity you don't know Greek any better. It's a marvelous story." Then he began telling me the story of Ulysses, which he himself could not read—he had vaguely heard Homer's name but he didn't know the story. But kids were bringing their lesson books back in the evening and he was engulfing the story. It struck me so forcibly because I had the translation by T. E. Lawrence, and I had two other versions right there in the house and we were always having a look at them just to compare daily life in modern Greece with daily life in ancient Greece, and I was always struck by the degree to which we found everything up to date. I don't believe a place like Ithaca, for example, has changed at all since Ulysses went back there. I certainly spent a few weeks there in exactly the sort of conditions that Ulysses must've found. But now, of course, the end is near at hand because last year they got television. (I wasn't joking. I like television and it wasn't a snide remark.) But when you have village manners and village customs with all the tremendous tradition and hospitality and a perfectly formal way of looking at things, town manners imposed on you by a box, which naturally entices you with the things it has to offer, naturally alter the old stately easygoing ways. It's done it to us all. It's done it to all our countries. And up to now it hasn't been possible in all those mountains in Greece to get a decent television service working. But the Greeks being ingenious have managed it, and I'm afraid it's going into action now, which means that all those very remote little villages which one used to know will now be glued to Athens. And of course Athens contains everything meretricious that London and New York can provide for it in terms of modern Greece. So inevitably it will have a radical effect on Greek manners of the old style. So this is why perhaps it's a bit nostalgic, my reminiscences of that forgotten Greece. For example, the monuments were not ringed about. I have slept for a whole month in a sleeping bag on Sunion and watched every dawn come up icy with dew. I slept inside the lion gate at Mycenae and among the statues of Olympia. There was no tourism then and there was no money to be had from monuments. In fact, in Olympia when I asked for the museum curator he came down on a bicycle, climbed into a tree and took the key down and opened the front door of the museum for me, and when we'd had a good look 'round he climbed into the tree and replaced the key. I could have pinched the lot. It was so easygoing and so Irish and absolutely unpretentious that one felt very much at home.

And then there were other extraordinary matters like those recounted by Ralf Brewster, who died recently, and who wrote two or three good books about Greece. When he was a student he was studying in Austria, he went down and spent a summer in the islands—he spoke good Greek—in a *caïque*. And in Siphnos one afternoon they found the museum wide open and the guardian asleep under a tree. He just said, "Go on, have a look around." So Ralf looked around and there was a beautiful little statue of a Pan lying on its back among the nettles in the garden, completely untended. And Ralf, who suffered from cupidity like us all, picked it up and put it in a shopping basket and carried it back to the *caïque* and took off with it for Austria. Well, nothing was heard of this loss for a little while, but the curator must've noticed it was missing and unluckily for Ralf, they suddenly discovered it was one of the most celebrated examples of its period. It appeared as an illustration in all the history books and it was really a national trophy that the Greeks couldn't afford to part with. They traced it to this youthful criminal—he was then a student at the university—and they threatened all kinds of actions against him, through the Austrian government. He probably risked a prison sentence, and he had to return this thing. Well, he returned it and he was blackmarked and couldn't go to Greece for five years after that. But when the sixth year came he managed to get a visa and he went back and in passing Siphnos again, out of curiosity he called in to have a look at the museum and he couldn't find this trophy anywhere in the museum and said, "Oh well, they must've taken it to Athens." Then he went outside in the garden and there it was in the same place, lying in the bushes where he'd found it first. On its back.

In this tiny community—it was a hamlet of about four houses—we had one doctor who was highly eccentric, who wasn't a doctor at all. In the town of Corfu there were some highly trained medical people and a good surgical laboratory, a good hospital and people trained at places like Edinburgh and in Paris, but in this tiny hamlet there was one old doctor on a bicycle. At the end of the war with the Turks there was a great shortage of doctors so the Greeks took all the pharmacists in Athens and created them doctors and sent them to the front. Then afterwards you couldn't take away their license to practice, so there were a great number of elderly men practising quite *ad hoc* in all these villages. And then there were the women bone-setters and herbalists who were much better than the old men and the only other literate person was Niko, the village schoolmaster. And a delightful priest who was extremely drunk most of the time. But he used to give tremendous services and excommunicate everyone from time to time and then take them back, you know. It was a small community and very tightly knit. I should suppose that you would find in an Irish island or in the Isle of Aron something rather comparable. But meanwhile, as a poet of 21 or 22, I had the most extraordinary stroke of luck—in fact the more I think of it the more amazing it seems to me—for if you cut yourself off from the ordinary literary life with all the things it has to offer you and you decide to go sit on a Greek island you would never hope to have the sort of friends I as a boy of 22 acquired almost by divine accident. I was later to call them my uncles, none of them wicked, all of them good. I had two American uncles at that time. They didn't come at once. First, I had T. S. Eliot as a publisher who guided and helped a great deal and consoled me against the loneliness of living in such circumstances. It was beautiful but it was terribly lonely. And then Henry Miller started bombarding me from Paris with a great deal of encouragement and documentation and masses of ideas. He was full of energy and enthusiasm which were wonderful guidelines for a young man. And then the other two uncles were Greek. One of them was George Katsimbalis, the Colossus of Maroussi. And the other one was Seferis who won the Nobel Prize later on. The quality of their sort of life style was such that it couldn't help inspiring you. I remember Seferis as a diplomat saying to me one day, "You know the old story about the pearly gates and St. Peter—I was thinking of it today at this awful reception." He went on, "I was thinking that if when I went to heaven St. Peter asked me 'What the hell have you been doing with your life down there?' the only thing I could really point to excuse it was my poems, and they're not good enough." And then I remember Miller saying "You know I never really believed in my vocation as a writer but now I realize I'm a protected person." It does suggest an eye out for another kind of life. And so parallel to this rather rocky life I was living was a frightfully intense interior life which was centered more or less on trying to shape myself into some sort of artist. And these people stretched out hands—touch, touch—and I felt in contact, and it's quite marvelous to be in contact though you're quite on your own and far away. It's a privilege accorded to few people. And so when I met Miller in Paris I took him back to Corfu and he wrote this good book about it. And when I went to Athens I took up with Seferis and Katsimbalis and his strange friends—he had a sort of Wuthering Heights of a house where numberless barrels of wine always seemed to be leaking all over everything. And on this creaky balcony, first weekend in Athens that I was there, I took Miller and Seferis and Katsimbalis and two other writers met in the evening to read verses. It was extremely memorable because the reading got steadily thicker and thicker because of the *retsina*, which was extremely powerful. And at night our wives came and fanned us with leaves and implored us to stop. In those hard Attic nights, Miller, I think has given the best description of them, the extraordinary dry heat—you're panting on the one hand because it's hot and yet on the other hand you're not sweating.

It's most extraordinary. You can walk at night with a clear electrical feeling. The actual violet of the dusk and the actual violet light which seems to play about Greece is something that's always impossible to describe. We've all tried it. It doesn't work in words and I don't think it works in paint really. It's a very peculiar thing. If you ask yourself, for example, what is Greece that Italy isn't, or Spain isn't, it's just precisely that curious magnetic violet X-ray dancing light, and I suppose also the feel always of water, either spring water, which you need urgently because you're like a thirsty dog in summer—even the electric light bulbs in a café give off so much heat that you can hardly stand them. You have to turn them off. And it's the water and it's the feeling of the light winds that girdle the Aegaen group of islands, which makes the nights delicious, particularly delicious, and the afternoons, with the good sailing wind that comes, the *meltemi*, and which sinks at dusk and allows you to bring boats in harbor perfectly calmly and sit down and watch everything settle into a pool of liquid. Cool nights, terrific stars, and heavy dew condensing like Scotch mist on your blanket. Into the sea at six, like diving into a mirror.

The poets themselves, particularly the country poets, have wonderful metaphors for the star display that comes immediately after the falling of the deep dusk. For the Milky Way they say that it's like scattered flour and for the other stars—and such a display of stars those of you who've been to Greece will know what I'm talking about—simply breathtaking—they say it's like a branch of an almond tree, a wreath of almond blossom, raised upon the night. Well, together with these poets I also met very briefly, and I can't claim to know him very well, the author of *Zorba*, Kazantzakis, and a highly dramatic, flamboyant poet called Sikilianos who, with his American wife, reinvented the festival of Delphi, which for nearly 20 years was one of the most singularly spectacular festivals of Greece, and really put cultural Greece on the map. And he was a very amusing, delightful and enormously flamboyant poet of the old school, very theatrical. I heard an anecdote which illustrates that particular kind of Greek temper. One night he was dining with Seferis, my friend, Kazantzakis and himself in a little tavern near Mycenae, and he was saying how really the poet could do anything, there was simply nothing that was beyond his powers. And that Jesus was a poet and that he,

Sikilianos was also a poet and that really if the poet had the thing in him he could even raise the dead. Miracles like that were no surprise. Well, he was talking in this vein and the innkeeper came out and said to him, "A chap just died upstairs, perhaps you would like to try." Well, Sikilianos is not the sort of person to be put off by that at all—he said, "What a good idea, I'll try; you'll see." And so he went upstairs. They didn't know what he did, perhaps he murmured. Perhaps he recited poetry; they heard all sorts of incantations and so on. And finally he came down and said, "He's so damned obstinate."

Now what I did was to bring along a few old and somewhat faded pictures from my scrap book in the hope of making this talk a bit actual, of illustrating it with places and faces. Well, when I asked the backroom boys to knock me up some lecture slides they looked at the quality of my prints and burst into tears. But I pinned my faith to the fact that after all this was an advanced technological institute and therefore able to perform wonders—after all, these were the people who were keeping Skylab in the sky. Surely they could keep poor Durrell talking? My faith was not misplaced; they dried their tears and got to work, and the magnificent results, many in color, you will see right now. So without more ado let us unleash the artwork. Behold!

Taken by the village photographer during my first year in Corfu. Second from left my landlord, on extreme right myself next to his wife.

The temple of Delphi where you make your big wish.

Niko, who sails like a demon and taught me Demotic Greek.

These marvelous monks combed their beards and sang Gregorian chants.

Well, now, this is the white house about which I was talking. Corfu town is in the distance there. It's a good 2½ hours on *caique*. And this little white house is the place where I lodged on this promontory here which is directly facing Albania, and where at night you get the most extraordinary displays. For example, in the autumn a kind of bacteria which I'm sure you must know, is washed up into the sea. The sea becomes thick and curdled and when you dive into it you're set on fire. I mean, you're not scorched or anything, but this animal, I've forgotten it's name, it throws out sparks so that when three or four people dive in you see figures of flame going into the water and off that point at night so frequently in the autumn we did that wondering why we weren't burnt because if you open your eyes you really do think you're going to be scorched.

Here's a closeup of the house and a bad picture of the *caique* coming to take them off, and that's my landlord up there looking wistful, I don't know why. This was taken much later. I lived on the top floor and the family lived on the bottom floor, and we had a boat which since has sunk, which used to be attached in that boat house. In winter the sea was so rough that it really came up to that balcony and swamped it. We had to completely tear away the vine and everything there. And it's very amusing. Now it's a place of pilgrimage. The Club Mediterranee charged people enormous sums to go look at it as the Durrell residence and serve them Coca-Cola for even larger sums. I don't know how posthumous you can feel, but my brother and I put on dark glasses and funny hats and we went on one of these trips, and I've never heard so much misinformation about our family and in such strange French. I think they were all Syrians. Anyway, we drank Coca-Cola in our own honor and sneaked off back to town.

There is a very pleasant fancy which is a far eastern one, namely, that you have two birth-places. You have the place where you were really born and then you have a place of predeliction where you really wake up to reality. One day you wake up and it's there, and in your inner life, in your dreams and so on and so forth, it's the place of predeliction that comes forward and which nourishes you. It's particularly useful in yoga to realize the difference between the two birthplaces. This my predeliction place. It's a shrine of St. Arsenius. He's a funny old cross-eyed saint, nobody knows much about him. He has brief mention in the calendar, but an ikon was washed up here after a storm. Naturally, a fisherman found it and decreed that it had to be housed properly, so the priest came and they built this little shrine for him and we found when we got here that this is one of those wonderful places. There's a very deep rock pool here and a cave about as big as a stage opening through a flue on the other side so it's fully lighted with a little pebble beach inside and reached by ducking under that lintel you find yourself in this extraordinary cave. We built a huge statue there in clay every year when we were there but in the winter the sea gets up and it licks out the cave like a hollow tooth and the statue just disappeared. Well now this is the place where I finished the *Black Book* and where my first poems were being selected when I was really working properly and beginning to feel my feet as a writer. It is also the place where we bathed naked all the time. We were extremely careful not to offend susceptibilities in Greece, and they were exteremely proper, the peasant girls and so on, so we didn't do ony of the idiocies you see Swedes doing now, running about Athens all naked. It brings great shame and discredit on our nations when we do that. Anyway, we were very careful about their susceptibilities, but we used to bathe there because those rocks completely prevented anyone from getting near the place. In fact I finished the *Black Book* naked one day, and then later on when the war came I got a letter from a friend of mine in the British Embassy in Athens saying, "What sort of orgies are you having up there?" This puzzled me a great deal. The war was just being declared and I didn't pay much attention, but I was living with my wife, legitimately married to her in a hamlet of four people and no orgies whatsoever, there was hardly enough to drink. And working every day at the shrine. What had happened was this. When I got to Athens and was taken on to the staff of the British Embassy I discovered a report by the local consul, who was a Greek, against me saying that I bathed naked with a woman. Now what happened was the British fleet used to visit the town 20 miles away and on Sundays they used to invite visitors aboard to have a look at the ships and during this one of the prize things to show was the range-finders of HMS Barham with a 25 mile range and they picked us up sitting there like Adam and Eve, and so the consul who was

My second birthplace, the shrine of St. Arsenius.

The Ionian Bar on Rue de Rivoli—the happiest drinks, warmest sunlight. . .

With Katsimbalis in Athens.

deeply shocked wrote a confidential report on me.

That's Niko, the sailor, and that's his boat, just a little rig, old-fashioned *caïque*, moves like honey. He's still there and he's still sailing like a demon. I saw him a couple of years ago and he's still speaking a very personal French. He's the man who showed me all these new books, the Demotic versions of Homer, which so touched me. I owe my first lessons in Greek to him and many is the drink we had under that vine. That's his house, actually, it's right alongside mine, and that's the morning *caique* coming in and that's some unidentified child who doesn't look at all pleasant.

This man in the foreground is the man who shows you around and pours out the Coca-Cola with a trembling hand and says that'll be 5 drachmas, but the place is still ravishing. You see how bright the mountain is behind it, it goes up in sort of leaps, really, to the crown and it's all self-seeded cypresses, marvelous olives amazingly tended considering the difficulties and that's the total crop. The main road moves there, but it's washed out immediately when the first rains come in winter and then the sea knocks out all the *caïque* stuff and really, to walk to town would take you, I suppose, 8 hours, which is difficult in cases of illness.

If you ever need any instruction about, or exactly how the Bible was considered and founded, these monks in Parakastrisa were absolutely marvelous. One of them spoke French; in those days my Greek wasn't up to it, but I did so admire their hats and I had all sorts of questions which later I was able to put more clearly in Greek in Alexandria to the patriarch there, but they were so gracious and kind and they loved having their photographs taken. It was very amusing, every time you produced a camera they would whip out combs and fix up their beards and hair and a religious service was wonderful. Their deep, growling Gregorian chant was like a deep sea moving over pebbles or a dry riverbed. They were all courtesy and kindness because we were then among the very few strangers in Greece, we were really a rarity and an oddity and we profited by that. Hospitality was absolutely wonderful. That hasn't changed—nor will it ever.

That's my bay and that is the old *"dogana"* or customs house where Albanian brigands used to be frisked before being turned loose in the island. Albania's only about 4 miles over by water at the narrowest point in the north and we used to go over very frequently in the winter and shoot with my shot-mad brother, my insect-mad brother was too young, and we never allowed him to touch anything that might go off. But he used to come here on one of these craft—these are island craft—camp the night with us and we'd go off with one of these things and he would go off after wild boar. There was plenty of mallard, very good duck shooting and he did a lot of boar shooting in Butrinto. This was long before Albania got it's own iron curtain. The calm at night was so extraordinary and then you'd hear suddenly in the olives a pipe just wheedling, just wheedling very softly and the tinkling of sheep bells. This girl used to bring her sheep down every morning and every evening walk along here.

This is my godson, he's called George—Jorgos. He's now 45 and has gigantic set of whiskers and he's got 2 children of his own and he's doing the Yokohama run taking wood from the Greek merchant marine to some point in China, I think. I put him in there for one good reason. It's a cautionary tale. The first thing Greeks do when they like you is to ask you to be a godfather. It's a friendly thing and an easy thing, but it's very much more serious than it is in our case because the laws of consanguinity are involved. In other words, if you baptize a boy and then you baptize a girl and they fall in love, they can't marry, they're just like real brother and sister. So, the thing, the tactic to adopt is to baptize only boys or only girls, and so I stuck to only boys and all my friends followed suit, but that way we've never caused any heartbreak at all.

This is a family shot. This is my shot-mad brother. These are all characters from my brother's book. There's my mother looking a bit frisky—looking a little bit sad, actually. That's Patrick Evans who writes poetry and was my brother's tutor. That's me trying to pretend I'm Byron, and that's Spiro, the great fixer, the man with the raucous voice. And that's my brother, the other brother is collecting insects just behind that shelf. That's my wife and that's a Swedish friend who I think got drowned. I don't know.

This is a very rare picture. You will never come across this again in your life. In the island of Corfu the patron saint, you probably know quite a lot about him already, his name is St. Speridian, all the children are named after him, but he's a great

Procession of the mummy of Saint Speridian, the miracle-maker.

The start of a wonderful book. Miller and the Colossus of Maroussi setting out.

miracle maker and a miracle-bringer. He can bring rain, he can do almost anything that you can think of. He actually is a real mummy and he's kept in the church of St. Speridian in a jeweled casket and once a year he's paraded around the town to bless all the people and to have a service and then he's put back. I have actually seen him and he's a genuine dried mummy, but this is very difficult to get a view of him in the general press and this as you see, my marvelous Rolliflex managed to do many many years ago.

Among all the muddles and the mysteries of this enchanting island this is an ordinary picture postcard of the Rue de Rivoli in Corfu. You see, I don't know what happens to people, but the various conquerers of the island fell dead asleep the minute they arrived there. The British arrived and they set up a very handsome government house, imitation of Malta, in red Malta stone and then they went to sleep. Then the French arrived and they said listen, this could easily be a little Paris, couldn't it? And so they started on the Rue de Rivoli which ends just at the end of that arcade there and they fell asleep, but meanwhile, the Arcades in good Italian Levantine style got taken over by bars, and that is the Ionian Bar where you can have the happiest drinks in the warmest sunlight in the most melodious fashion in the world today.

This should make your blood run cold. You wouldn't sit on an atom bomb and light a cigar, would you? This young poet so pleased with himself, what is he doing? He's leaning on the great *omphalos*, the great bellybutton of the world at Delphi. In those days, Delphi had no barbed wire around it and the *omphalos* was lying about in a field for anyone to sit on—I could have taken it home in the car if I could have lifted it. It's the ancient Greek center of the world and of course, all the more dangerous for a poet to do that sort of thing, to take up that blood-curdling arrogant attitude because right next door is the shrine with the Pythea where the goddess of all poetic inspiration officiates, and she could really have driven him mad. If she had turned over in bed he would have been crushed like a bed bug. She must have been asleep or away for the weekend when he did that. But I thought as sort of a cautionary tale, as a cautionary warning it was worth showing you that. Phew!

Here I am leaning on the *omphalos*, great bellybutton of the world.

And that's of course is where you make your big wish: that's Delphi. And that's the temple of Delphi, always the light warp of wind in the pines, that slow-moving strange feel of leaves going all the time and the wind on your cheek, which you feel everywhere in Greece. Dry wind, dry grass. It's not exactly refreshing, it's monitary, as though somebody were trying to whisper something to you. You feel it in Delos. You hear the reeds moving and you feel the wind on your cheek. And in Delphi where you have these great groves of pines up on the stadium you hear this—it's not quite sinister, but then when an eagle crosses the view and you hear the creak of its wings it matches with it and suddenly you feel your own breathing and you do understand what the Greeks meant by the panic sense. It's the sense of something really outside yourself that belongs to the place that seizes you. It's not altogether—well, I should say it could be fearfully disagreeable

Katsimbalis, the Colossus of Maroussi.

With Miller in California, 1973.

and frightening. You feel ancient Greek time passing. I've camped there in that place. It's not as frightening as Epidaurus, but it is a frightening place with its huge green valley and at night when the sun goes down it's astonishing in its deep fear really. You feel the presence of the Gods. That's why I'm so terrified when I see myself innocently sitting astride the *omphalos* up there like an idiot fiddling with the safety-catch of the universe. It really is terrifying.

This is the start of a wonderful book. It's a portrait of Henry Miller and the Colossus of Maroussi setting off for the trip which ended with the book so to speak. The Colossus is a much heavier man now. He was much slimmer then. And that's Miller. They're going down the steps of Ghika's house in Hydra and just about to step aboard the boat and then they disappeared and we saw them much later in Athens after all the adventures which Miller has recorded in his book had taken place. So it's rather a historic picture. I don't know whether Miller has a copy of it, I must try and get him one.

That was last year when I came. Considering his bad luck with his operations and with the state of his leg, all the more galling because this is a bicyclist, this is an athlete, you know how humiliating it is if you're an athlete to have anything wrong with you physically. The amazing thing is that his skull is full of ideas. He's painting watercolors, he's writing. He's now five chapters up on a new book. Even now, after a second and a very long painful operation I've never seen such courage and I've never seen such optimism. I learn a great deal every time I'm with him. We're hoping to have a big birthday party on Wednesday when he's got Anais Nin to come in and so the three Musketeers are going to settle down for a good French evening we hope.

Now this is the growling, bumbling man-mountain Katisimbalis walking around Athens. He's trying to convince me that I ought to translate Pope Joan and I'm saying, "No. It's a dirty book." He has a strong resemblance to two people whom perhaps you might know. If you happen to know the French film actor Raimu, he resembled him so much both in growl and in voice and in general disposition that when Raimu died the Greek press said, "Well, thank God we've still got our own version in Mr. Katsimbalis." But those of you who live here would probably understand better if I say that he is absolutely the image of a wonderful film actor called Sydney Greenstreet who also had a very deep slurring voice and also was rather grumpy and was always a sleuth of some sort or a detective. And indeed when Katsimbalis tried to come here to see Henry Miller he arrived in Los Angeles and went into a bar for a drink and a woman screamed, "Sydney!" and fell in a dead faint. He just caught her before she hit the ground and everyone in the bar was white. He tried to find out what this was about. Apparently Mr. Greenstreet had just died and had been buried that morning and they'd all just come back from his funeral when George walked in. There he is in a more characteristic vein. There he is in France. He's found the sort of wine that suits him. Very bad influence. Very bad influence.

Now, I don't know what sort of picture I've made, perhaps rather a muddled one of this scrapbook of impressions. It's so various and the country itself is so rich and so evocative that just to have spent one's youth there seems to be something that, well, it's pure gold. And the people who live there echo it too. Their hospitality, their kindness and all of the communities. Indeed, I was thinking of Parga and the little Turkish community. There was one small episode which may perhaps make you smile. In Parga the Americans were marketing a chocolate laxative, called X-Lax, I think, and they had translated their advertising into good Turkish, and the slogan for the advertising campaign was "It works while you sleep." Now, to the Turkish mind, that something should work while you are actually sleeping seemed absolutely wonderful and the sales of this chocolate probably still go on to this day under this excellent slogan. Well, of course, everyone likes something for nothing. I can think of a thousand more small anecdotes but they don't really add up to any conclusive sense. What really echoes on in the back of my mind is the place where I was reborn, where I finished the *Black Book* and was photographed by the British fleet in the state of nudity, that house with its remoteness and the islands going down like soft gongs all the time into the amazing blue, and I shall really never, never ever forget a youth spent there, discovered by accident. It was pure gold. But then of course there may be a little element of self-deception in it because youth does mean happiness, it does mean love, and that's something you can't get over.

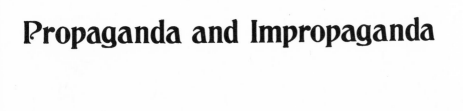

Propaganda and Impropaganda

I came to diplomacy very late and by accident and through the
back door: and had it not been for a sudden war erupting I
don't think I would have ever been interested in it and I don't
think it ever would have accepted me, for neither by birth, nor
education, nor upbringing am I the sort of person who might have
made the grade as a career diplomat before the war. And even if I
had wanted to do it and had tried, I think I would have failed the
examinations which were necessarily very hard and I would've
lost on all counts. But when the war broke out it suddenly became necessary for people who had languages to supplement the
relatively inane diplomatic corps which had a great deal of style
on the exterior but nothing much inside, and to help disguise the
fact that they were full of gingerbread. And so through the orifices
of the more modest but really professional consular service they
infiltrated a lot of people who knew something. I had the ill luck,
or the good luck, in Athens to be taken aboard simply because I
knew some Greek at that time: and could write.

It's not entirely the fault of the diplomatic service that it seems
so moribund, which it truthfully is a bit nowadays. There's always
a function for an embassy where you want, for example, to have
an intelligent and civilized discussion of fishing rights or to
elaborate a new treaty or something like that. But what's really
made diplomacy moribund today is really the telegram and the
telephone and the communications set up. Nothing is really more
moving, as for example in Government House Cyprus or in any
embassy, than the bound file of the reports and dispatches by the
ambassador 50, 60, 80 years ago which were all carefully hand-
lettered by his scribes, carefully corrected and in numberless copies
were then dispatched for distribution. But by the time I reached

it these days were over. I was already 12 when I was sent to England, from India it took me a month to communicate with my parents by sea and during the early years there was no air service at all. The air connections started around 1932. When I was in Corfu at the very beginning of the war there was one old sea-plane which engineered the communications with India so that what with post office delays it really took 10 or 15 days for an airmail letter to get to India. Well, you can imagine if you have a very violent situation on your hands as an ambassador has frequently and might have to act and invoke or threaten, you haven't time to ring up Whitehall about it. Well now Whitehall opens the daily newspaper and rings you up and tells you what to do, so naturally you feel rather on the shelf all the time. But in the old days it was very much up to you to take a decision on the spot and to act and to put up with the consequences if you were in the wrong afterwards. So it gave a backbone to people like Burton and so on. As consular officials and as diplomats were working in an excellent tradition, they felt functionally that their role was an important one. It's less important today, and with the advent of so much nonsense about spying it's become increasingly tricky. But relatively speaking I very much admire the old type of diplomat, many of whom I worked under when I was a junior in their embassies, who belonged to the Burton strain and who one could see the relationship with, for example, Sir Thomas Wooton who was probably a friend of Shakespeare (he wrote excellent poetry) and who announced that he had taken Venice for his consulate and when asked what he did said "I lie abroad for my country." Of course "lying" means also in Elizabethan "I reside abroad", but the doubletake is there because "lying" also means "lying", and there was a good element of need at that moment what with the battle between Protestantism and Catholicism on the continent and the Armada approaching and so on, that somebody should have his lies ready in his bag, and good ones.

And then of course there was the great Tallyrand who's probably the greatest diplomat of all. You know it's customary before you're sent out to your first post to have ten minutes with the Secretary of State. It's like baptism or circumcision. It's terrifying for him and for you equally. You don't know what to say and so he has a tendency to say, "Well, uhum . . . Durrell, you're going to . . . uhum . . .you're going to Athens, I think." "Yessir." "Well, the ambassador is so and so and so . . ." What he doesn't say is that the ambassador is an idiot, that his wife looks disastrous and that he's socially really hopeless, and that you'll have to use all your tact to get your job done without offending them. He can't say that naturally, but he coughs and sputters breathes on you and off you go. Well Tallyrand developed this farewell technique to a fine art and when his young attaches were being posted, he always stopped them as they opened the door and were saying goodbye with the phrase, *"Et surtout par trop de zele."* "And whatever you do, not too much zeal." Which, of course, was quite right. You see, the only good diplomatic advice is to (a) shut up and (b) don't do a thing, because fundamentally it's really good Zen, it's really good Taoist advice because in the final analysis you can't do anything. Events are always moving far too fast, the personalities involved are far too unimaginative and silly, and everybody's been carried away on a tide of absurdity so that really, though it sounds frivolous, but the best thing to do is to sit tight. You are dealing with maniacs and nuts so naturally the situations are nutty.

Of course in my particular department it was one of the things we couldn't do because I was always posted to crisis spots where sitting tight was just not on because one was always being invaded by Russians or Germans or something like that . . . But I always remembered the remark about excessive zeal and I always tried to follow it to the best of my ability. And where it was possible to let my colleagues make mistakes, I let them do it. I never won any decorations out of this meritorious business but in fact I didn't put up, as they say in the service, many "bad blacks." And my memories of diplomatic life are coloured always by embassies with an enormous fire going in the garden. When the enemy are arriving you burn everything marked "Top Secret" and everything is. I think I've been in more retreats than you can possibly imagine.

I'd hardly been taken on in Athens when the Germans nearly arrived. They were 40 miles away, and they had discovered that tanks could come down the railways, they didn't need the roads. We'd blown up all the roads, of course, but had forgotten the railways. They'd put 50 tanks on the railways and the next thing we knew there were sign posts telling them "Athens 5 miles." So, naturally, we had to get out very very fast. Well, this always is a marvellous situation because in diplomacy to add to your own importance you mark everything highly confidential and secret because this means that your bureau is sort of upgraded, so consequently you have an immense amount of documentation, most of it from the Encyclopaedia Brittanica and the Guide Bleu, and Mrs Beeton's which is all marked secret and confidential and it's essential to burn this because you mustn't let it fall into German hands. When a British embassy is leaving the first thing you see is a gigantic bonfire with all the attachés, looking like attachés usually look, with kerosene cans dousing manuscripts and a huge plume of smoke going up. It's a heartening sight. Well, Athens was my starting point in retreating and I've been retreating ever since until I ended up last week in Pasadena. My back is against the wall now. I'm at Caltech at the moment defending culture, whatever that is.

But the Athens episode was particularly instructive because we had an extremely bright military attaché who had not respected Tallyrand's famous advice to his secretaries. He was full of zeal, too full of zeal, and we had far too many documents marked confidential, secret, highly this, highly that and the other, and the garden was full of them. So he put them all in a van. He said, "I have an idea," he didn't tell anyone what it was. He took them round to the local crematorium. Now, the Greeks are mad about machinery, but they don't understand it very well. They had just got a brand new crematorium. The chap, who bought it on a purely commercial basis, was being excommunicated by the archbishop who didn't believe in burning bodies. But the thing was there and working intermittently. The military attaché took all our scret and confidential documents down there. He put them into one of the crematories and pulled the lever. Unfortunately, something went wrong. The Greek attendant had in some curious way fixed the draught at a wrong angle, and all this half-charred stuff flew out of the main central flue and all over Athens, it was like a snowstorm. I was walking in Athens waiting for some transport so I could run away to the sea, and I saw things coming out of the sky. They were half-charred bits of paper like this piece with dispatches beginning "following from Churchill to Lord Halifax" . . . And all over the place there were *drifts*. But as it always happens in grave cases, people never realise when something is given to them, just as they didn't realise the date of the Normandy landings, when they were given them by a spy in Turkey. So when the Germans came all this paper was swept up. Nobody read a single word. The whole war policy, American, British and everything else was outlined in the secret and confidential information which flew out through the flue and descended like a snowstorm.

That is why too much zeal, you see, ruins the whole shoot. The eager attaché fortunately redeemed himself by becoming a great commando and was much decorated. He's now a very distinguished war historian. But we had so much trouble with zealots. In the old days of Sir Henry Wooton it could've been much different, owing to distance and lack of instant Whitehall interference. Later on, in Egypt, I met Noel Coward who had gotten so sick of this kind of rubber stamp secrecy that he had a huge one made for his manuscript which read "Highly Trivial." But this is the mere farcical end of diplomacy. It has other more serious functions.

Nowadays what is valuable, and what I did see actually in close action as a perfectly valid operational technique is clever bargaining. Another useful thing you can do is to correctly evaluate personalities in terms of what they might or might not do; and one of the things that the ambassador who's sensitive and clever, on-the-spot, since he has access to let's say Archbishop Makarios or Tito or Farouk—(three cases I'm thinking of)—his dispatches are important for the Secretary of State so that he can judge whether to press a little in this way or that way to bring about the desired result. That is something that can't be done by television or by long distance telephone. So in that sense, and in the commercial and political sense, diplomacy still has its place though it's a very wearisome occupation. I found it terriby wearying, but I never wasted it in the sense that I was always buoyed up by the feeling that I must make notes the whole time for my novels.

I took a leaf out of the notebook of the man I admire most as a novelist, Stendhal, who was also stuck as a minor consular official all over the globe, but who never relented. And it is very important to know how an ambassador behaves when he's hysterical. If you've helped one on and off with his overcoat for a long time you really do get the feel. In a novelist who's trying to describe embassy life or what it's like in Buckingham Palace, if you haven't been there it's extremely hard to get away with it. Something hollow in the tone looks through. So in a sense, if I need an embassy I know where to go now. I've got three. One ambassador more foolish than the next. One a real genius of foolishness but a marvellous writer who really did the best paper on Tito's psychology ever. If he hadn't been a nut he wouldn't have been able to understand Tito. But it was one of the most delicate and penetrating performances of evaluating whether Tito was going to go back in the fold or whether he was going to stay out on the Balkan wing as an independent and what sort of temperament he had. Really it was a brilliant psychological thing. That was Sir Charles Peake who died recently, and who was one of the vaguest men I ever met. Every time he came to see me in my office he patted a bicycle which was in the hall and said, "Hey, Budgin, how are things down in the cipher room?" In fact, I can assure you that all Evelyn Waugh had to say about diplomats in "Black Mischief" is absolutely dead true. As for Sir Charles, whom I came to love, he could also sit in a chair with his lips working, opposite me at my desk, tearing up paper into smaller and smaller bits, and after three-quarters of an hour say, "Yes. That's what we'll do," and walk out without telling me what the devil it was we must do.

But he was good. I did a paper which was received rather coolly when I left from the man who was going to inherit my post. It was called "Propaganda and Impropaganda." Part of what I'm telling you today was in it. It was how, just as in business, you should know your victim, so to speak, so in propaganda you should either know the language of the person you're dealing with or something about his beliefs and views so that you can influence him. Later in the war we got very skillful and we caused numberless suicides among the Japanese by printing a poem, an extraordinary, simple haiku poem with a moon and the Yellow River or something like that. Whole regiments surrendered in tears with this thing. It was done, of course, by a Japanese. No Englishman would've found it possible to do. At the very outbreak of the war in Cairo when I arrived there, the British community, to show their patriotism, had done something so foolish that I can hardly bear to speak about it. They printed a poster of a bulldog with a British flag 'round its neck and the slogan, "Who is for liberty, Who is for victory?." Now, at first sight it seems a very harmless thing, but the worst insult in Arabic is "dog". And this was done by people who had been residents in Egypt for half a lifetime. They should have known that "ya kelb" is the worst insult an Arab can give or take. It would be like, you know, the French being particularly sensitive to being compared to pigs— "cochon" is the worst insult in French. Can you imagine at the beginning of an important war like that putting out a poster of a pig with the French flag around its neck and saying "Let's all be patriotic pigs together for victory."? You wouldn't get a Frenchman to rally to that. Well, naturally, the English couldn't understand why the Arabs were rolling about with laughter in the street when they saw this thing. And this was just the beginning of our war effort.

Diplomats speak good French in general, but owing to the rapid shift around they are limited: two years is just not enough to deal with a complicated language like, for instance, Japanese. In the old days you were more or less projected forward toward a country, often of your own choice. You were told, "Will you do five years in Japan?", and you were given a handsome allowance and a Japanese instructor to teach you the language. So those in the old colonial service were all the experts; they knew the country with all its personalities, and got to love it very much. They were quite a different breed from modern diplomats who have spent two years here, two years there; and the service is more picturesque than really serious. Also it's taken less seriously because of this element. I'm thinking, for example, of Sir Charles Bell's mission to Tibet. No one had ever been to Tibet after Younghusband had conquered it in 1904. We established diplomatic ties with it and then Bell took a small group in, a chancery of five members. The first thing they noticed was that drink and cigarets were offensive to Buddhists. So the rule went out that there was one room in the Embassy where you could smoke a cigaret or have a drink; but to all intents and purposes they would never drink or smoke outside the premises, and certainly never in public.

And owing to that one small consideration Bell became very friendly with the Dalai Lama and secured all the trade negotiations going at that time. He also secured all our supply lines up to the north—just one of one simple, tactful act. And that works even today.

The other day I was in Geneva and ran across a man whom I think I call "Hoyle" in one of my books. He's a very venerable chap now in UNESCO who speaks beautiful Turkish and beautiful Greek, and has been in East Bahan for a hundred years—knows everybody, all the personalities, and is very gentle and sweet. And he said, "You know, I've got so bored with Geneva, not only the climate but also work in the U.N. is absolutely asinine—anybody would be qualified to do it. You have no idea how useless one feels as a diplomat. So I think that I'm going to the Congo, I see there's a job going there." And I said, "But listen, have you seen the evening's paper?" He said, "Oh you mean about them eating the last mission?" I said, "Yes, you know the Balubas—they're turning everybody into soup. You don't want to go in there." And he said, "Well, to be eaten by a Baluba—at least one would feel that one had served some purpose."

But in justice to us, as usual, stag-legged and rather behind the times and really adrift, we hadn't realised what propaganda was, you see, far less what impropaganda was. We knew the word *agitprop* and vaguely we had in our minds a sort of historical perspective on propaganda in general, But the Germans had set us a particular case. They set up a ministry of lies, and they were pumping out, like a Barnum Circus of absolutely flat, bare-faced lies, and they suddenly realised that, like a television commercial, if you repeat it long enough people don't bother to question, they take it as true. We hadn't realised this. We lived in a democracy where most of us lied negatively, not really by open intention, but by simple evasion, really, and where a free press rapidly ventilates problems and queries, particularly in England where you feel that if you write to the *Times* the whole thing will be settled. Not in the new *Times*, the old *Times*. The one that's dead now, that you used to call "Auntie". This propaganda question was a sort of characteristic fixation on our part and we suddenly had a brilliant idea about five years before the war when Goebbels was in full flood with the German propaganda machine. We thought we ought to make a distinction between propaganda and culture, and surely cultural penetration is what we really needed, what we really wanted because it would bring together all the most erudite and most instructed people in any given foreign community with our own instructed. We'd mutually agree to lend books to the universities and so on. This is all very well. This society, which is rather like a missionary society, was founded after a lot of argument, and the Queen agreed to be a patron. But the thing got so delayed that it was only after the outbreak of the war that it was actually launched. And this happened to be one of the master strokes of our policy because all of a sudden in Athens, in a very difficult position, a whole lot of young men in white knitted wool ties with copies of Keats in their pockets, and civilians to boot, at a time when everybody else was in uniform, suddenly arrived in Athens, opened institutes and started instantly teaching English and teaching Keats. Well, the Germans realised at once that the entire British Secret Service was at work, doubled all their effectives and kept a watch night and day on these innocent schoolmasters. Being German, of course, everything normal was suspicious. Sometimes I myself wondered whether we hadn't been too clever and whether these teachers were not, after all, spies. Then when I joined them to give some lectures I realised it was the most innocent and absurd thing that could have happened. But they would choose the outbreak of the war to launch this organisation. It was called The British Council.

Naturally, the salaries were so low that the members were rather inferior. One had hopes that our general culture was going to be on a pretty high standard, but my boss for these lectures was sitting at his desk one day and asked me what I wanted to lecture about and I gave him some subjects which might please the Greeks when all of a sudden the accountant came in absolutely white and said "There is 10,000 pounds missing from the safe, sir." This man, who was a clergyman said, after a moment of blankness, "Oh yes, my goodness, I think I have it here." And he *had*. He had it all in his pocket. He had forgotten. He transferred all the petty cash to his pocket and he was only interested in ancient history. He was working on a book about Herodotus. And so the entire funds were in his pocket—I was horrified too because my salary was coming out of it. And then in Egypt I went 'round to see the British Council representative to find out if they'd like any lectures that could be done for the Middle East, political ones especially, and I met an extraordinary man, very gloomy, who said, "Where would you like to live if you really wanted to live somewhere, old man?" So I said, "Well, really, there's only place I really want to live. That's in France." He said, "Why France?" I said, "Well, I can give you a number of reasons, but just take the simplest . . . food." He said, "I thought you'd say that." Then he said, bitterly, "Do you know I've crossed France frequently and I always carried my food in a paper bag because I was so badly swindled one day at lunch I decided I was never going to pay for another French meal?" And this man was our cultural representative! Needless to say I didn't go any further with this thing at all. I went back to the embassy and I stayed there.

I should perhaps say a few words about the functions of embassies and the role they play; in our crazy spy-mad age the whole question of information has been much bedevilled by the fact that all information of whatever kind has been lumped together by the spy-nuts behind the Curtain and made to sound as if it were military in scope. This is plain madness. When an embassy is appointed to a country it is perfectly normal for them to find out what is going on there, what personalities rule there, in the simple interests of business or cultural association. Of course when some countries are acting in bad faith and with bad intent their consciences prick them for they know that they are building a secret army or secret airforce and they don't want the fact known. But the whole domain of commercial and cultural relations is helped or hindered by the knowledge of a good embassy. They study the produce of the country and put people in their own country in touch so that business deals can be arranged. They send poets and journalists and painters on short visits. They arrange for painting or films to be shown reciprocally. All this is for the best, and only in this lunatic age would it be thought of as spying. But when countries have something to hide, particularly the communist countries, and you get a spy phobia, it's very amusing to see what is regarded as spying: all these legitimate activities which in peace time or under normal diplomatic arrangements wouldn't be considered at all reprehensible, but in fact helpful information. For example, here I wouldn't have to bug you for information about silkworms or about San Francisco wines; I would just ring up the board of trade and go out and get all the information I needed and send it home clear, not in cipher. Whereas, half the trouble with this problem is that what is not really spying is considered spying. For example, I spent $4\frac{1}{2}$ years in Yugoslavia for my sins; that was tough. There everything was considered spying, even breathing. When you arrived at the gate you practically have a man to breathe for you, to breathe down you and on you. And when you went to the embassy he breathed on your car, and when you came out he followed in another car. And then there was a man in your house who breathed on you too. That's how I'm so good at yoga now because I learned breathing from the secret police there. But it was perfectly foolish also, because the amount of information you can get if you really want to out of censored papers is absolutely marvellous if you know a little bit of Freud, a little bit of crossword puzzle, a little bit of this and that. The military attaché used to have great fun because he could read Yugoslav, and reading the official communiques he could follow the movements of their units of the army all over the town. For example, the artillery was largely horse-drawn, so every time they arrived in a village they put an ad in the local paper asking for farriers to shoe their horses. Thus we always knew the 37th division was at this particular place because we used to buy all the papers, even the provincial ones. I mean, if they force you to work you can really find almost anything with a bit of logic and intuition. Meanwhile, they used to do silly things. They used to put microphones in the bowl of roses on your table. Whereupon we would tape the noise of lavatory chains and fill their mikes with long long strips of water music. We played this lavatory chains noise for hours to their mikes until they got tired and moved them.

All that's the rather futile and foolish end of diplomacy, but the serious end is fascinating, and it *is* interesting and it can be fruitful. As I say, acted on in good faith, it can be enormously useful between nations. It's a pity that communications have rendered it rather suspect and rather moribund because a great personality is still a great negotiator; and I have seen even very silly personalities—I would describe Sir Anthony Eden as rather a fop, but he's an extraordinarily good negotiator—and I saw him locking horns with a trade delegation in Yugoslavia and he was extremely bright. I wouldn't have suspected it from his political role. And then of course we had other problems because half the world is ruled by nuts as you probably know. Or do you know?

And then the evaluation of a very trick position between church and state, for example, in Egypt. In the middle of the war—the Egyptians had declared war but they didn't want to fight—they declared war because we asked them to. So we allowed them to man the anti-aircraft defenses of Cairo and Alexandria, which they did with considerable skill, but technically they were out of the war, so that their towns were not bombed, they were open cities. Now Farouk was a strangely divided character, very strange. On one hand rather civilised, on the other hand seething with Arab resentments, and like anyone who's been to British public school, pretty scratched up. It was even dues what he might elect to do. While we were fighting the Germans in the desert we couldn't really risk a political situation on an Arab basis in Egypt where, for example, the anti-aircraft defenses of Cairo might be withdrawn suddenly. It was not that the defenses themselves were so terribly important, but the towns would've been bombed and then the Egyptians would have panicked and we would have had an interior situation which would have bene-fited Rommel very much indeed. As it was, by a stroke of luck and a fluke, and some diplomacy, and the use of one tank it was stabilized. They went late one night and broke down the palace wall and told Farouk that he really must appoint Nahas Pasha who was pro-British and able to stabilize the situation. And he did do that, but he didn't like doing it at all and it was, I suppose, a bit of a fascist act. But he had no choice. We had to do that because at one point the Germans were 40 kilometers away and it was quite clear Rommel was going to reach Cairo that evening.

At this time I was attached to the British Embassy and was as usual pining for an independent command. I was always com-plaining about being under other peoples' orders. I was extremely independent and had a number of bad ideas which now, looking back, I am rather glad they didn't let me put into action. But one of the great tragedies in my life has been that whenever I did get an independent command it was in a situation which had gone

too far, had deteriorated into a crisis post. I arrived in Yugoslavia on the night Tito broke with Stalin. The frontiers were
humming with tanks. Then again when I got a post in Cyprus the
whole island went up under me, so to speak. Well, in Egypt, when
I finally did get my independent command, it was I think
because they thought I would arrive in Alexandria and find a
German sitting in my office chair. They realized that the only
man crazy enough to accept such an appointment was Durrell.
Why not give Durrell to the Germans? He was not much use to
us and could do us little harm if they took him away. But I was
so fed up with Cairo that I thought I would take a chance. So I
drew a revolver which I only knew how to fire very vaguely, and
climbed into the night train for the coast. It was all blacked out,
very sinister; and from time to time there were halts, mysterious
unexplained halts, in the desert; everything went dead silent.
Only giant mosquitoes filled the carriages, biting us to death.
When I arrived in my post Rommel was still 40 kilometres away;
his troops had got bogged down in a bottleneck of sand dunes and
lakes called the Qattara Depression. I couldn't believe my luck.

In Alexandria everything was shut up. When there's
an element of panic in the air the first sign you
notice is all the cafés close and all the delicatessens
and everything like that, and they roll down those iron
shutters; and the more intelligent had actually put up signs saying
"Welcome to Rommel" in German. Well, I went around and
made a complete list of these people. It took me about three hours
and then I went to the British H.Q. and said, "If Rommel doesn't
arrive tonight, these people are going to be out of bounds to British
troops, I assure you." And the Army agreed and they stayed out
of bounds for four months. Finally, I had delegations of these
people coming to my office and pleading to be put back on the
visitor's list because after Rommel was repulsed and the British
got back into Alexandria these people found the British soldiers
couldn't drink in these places. It was out of bounds for them. So
this was the only practical thing I could do in the way of propaganda. I made a lot of friends this way.

But the first night was a frightfully exciting night because in
Cairo I went down to Operations in a great big gloomy hall with
a giant board which marked all the positions.

The scale was so great that you could almost see individual units, and I went down with a friend of mine who ran one of the Four Hurricanes out of Crete, Dudley Honor. He said, "Come out and have a look and let's see because I think tonight's the night." And the trains were taking everybody away, sending off all the women and children. A delicious thing to experience actually. Pure vertigo of panic in the streets. And on this operations board in this absolutely silent room, the tapes were marking this thing, the Qattara Depression; the chips were down, Rommel was closing in, and we knew there was just one tarmac road and no further to go. Nothing to stop him except sand dunes. And all of a sudden about 2:00 in the morning the chap takes his earphones off and says, "We've advanced a bit," then marked up three positions in the neck of the depression which were considered really unassailable by us. Of course Rommel had a lack of equipment and he also had the long lines of communications. We took an enormous deep breath and went out and had a drink and I wrote up the names of all these dogs who had said "Welcome Rommel," and for about two months British soldiers really didn't drink there and they sobbed their little hearts out until I asked the Army to relent.

And then technology also has its problems. In fact it creates more than it solves. One of the great things that bugged me as a press attaché always when I had to try to control newspapers was misprints. The Arabs just loved them. The English-speaking paper in Cairo, the Egyptian Mail, was manned by an Arab staff. The three proofreaders were absolutely grey, they were little grey old men. They'd got grey trying to correct misprints. And the Arabs were an anarchic lot who didn't understand what they were setting up. The linotypist seemed to be playing the organ the whole time. And as fast as you sent down one proof with some misprints on it, they sent you back a whole new set of misprints and this could go on indefinitely. Of course, it led to awful political situations. For example, there was a particularly good and devout general who was described in the Egyptian Mail as a "bottle-scarred" veteran instead of a "battle-scarred" veteran. His press attaché rang me up at the embassy and said, "Look, it's absolute scandal that General B. should be treated like this. You must get a correction." So I rang up Mr. Goldstein who was the head of the paper and I said, "Do you realise what you've done to General B.? Will you please correct this tomorrow morning?" He said yes, he would and the next morning they come out with "We are so sorry about the reference to a "bottle-scarred veteran", what we mean was a "battle-scared veteran." There seemed to be no way forward from this. I was on the point of resigning.

Then there were all kinds of engaging things. When Lord Mountbatten came to visit us he was described as having a lovely "louse-lipped smile." And the British Air Force was going to get even with Germany with their giant Sunderland Flying-Goats. You know their flying boats were quite celebrated, but their flying goats? Perhaps a secret weapon? A new British device to defeat the enemy, you see. And an item in the want-ad section of the paper, placed by a gentleman who needed someone to cook for him, read: "British officer urgently needs one good plain cock." We had a very great deal of trouble like this, which kept everyone swearing and telephoning.

And I've also had trouble with statistics. I tried first of all to computerise this job a little bit because we were wasting so much money and it was costing lives to bring newsprint across. One had to take it seriously. The newsprint shortage was such that shipping space was allocated out for various demands and it seemed to me scandalous that one should waste it on propaganda pamphlets describing the situation in Nubia. So I started doing some spot propaganda as market research, of the kind that I suppose the big industries here must do; in fact it's a kind of advertising, really. But so much was wasted that I tried to establish a kind of percentage of waste. I got one factory which had 2,000 workers and I inundated it with 2,000 pamphlets on one subject or another and I went on inundating it, and as we knew the dustmen in the area we collected what they threw away so that I finally established that most of the stuff I was feeding into the factory was being thrown automatically into the dustbin. By continuing the process I suddenly discovered that what creates a demand is shortage. I'm not a good Marxist, but I suddenly realised that if I gave 3% of the total, the fact that it wasn't enough to go around made the 3% read it and pass it around, whereas if I gave 100% of my product to them it appeared in the wastebins the next morning automatically. So this was a valuable discovery for the record. But I couldn't interest London in this. They thought I was being too clever. Of course suborning the press and buying its influence is also very gay but what can one do against honest people with honest convictions? Nothing. The Germans were much better at it because they were not so respectable and they were not worrying about their image the whole time because they were desperate. We were still fuddy-duddy and worrying a great deal about our image, so it was they who suborned all the *mullahs* in the minarets who give out the evening prayers and make a little sermon, to tell the Egyptians that once Rommel came they'd all have ice cream. And the Egyptians liked ice cream so much that this was our most dangerous moment, our most heroic moment. I was tempted to do a cut-rate ice cream act and hand out ice cream on our side, but this would have been considered rather inferior behaviour. But our servants at our houses came to us and said, "We're sorry you're leaving. You've been quite square with us and on the level, but this ice cream, you know, you can't pass that out." And it's very difficult in those sort of countries to find some way of countering that kind of idiocy. We came across it all the time, all over the place. And it was no good buying an indignant priest to say, "not ice cream but bully beef." We couldn't do that either. So I had a great deal of trouble with that.

And then there was my statistical plan—I'm warned forever against the reliability of statistics . . . When I was in Rhodes I had to run 3 newspapers, an English daily for the army, and an Italian daily for the Italian community and a little Turkish one. And I started a Greek one called "Kronos" which I believe is still going on, which was quite pleasant and had a little literary corner which the English thought was highly untrustworthy. Then I received my annual reports. My agent said the sales on a small island called Micronesium (one of the Dodecanse group), it's so tiny that it really hasn't got a name, was buying 400 copies of this newspaper. This was a bit of a puzzle. We were printing 5,000-10,000 copies, but 400! The total inhabitants of that island struck me as around 25. I couldn't understand why each man was reading my paper so often. I knew it was a good paper, I was putting my back into it, it was excellent stuff, but I didn't see why they would keep buying extra copies just to reread the same things? So I thought this merited a trip, and I got the navy to ship me out

In a corvette and I went ashore. I was met as though I was a sort of Henderson the Rain King. And only two people on the island read, the schoolmaster and the priest, and the others were all peasants. I said, "Of course, you read the news to them." They said yes. I said, "Where in the hell do these other 385 copies go then?" He said, "What a godsend, we use them to wrap fish. You know I can't tell you how much they mean to us." The whole of this little fishing industry was based on my journalism. It's a very salutory thought when you think statistically to remember that sort of thing because its puts you in your place. Don't ever trust statistics—even your own sales. They are really wrapping fish in your work.

Well, the great curse of diplomacy is, I think, national days. A great horror, particularly in peace time, because everyone has to have a national day birthday party and everybody has to go for fear of offending the Israelis, offending the Arabs, offending some-body, so you don't dare to offend somebody and so spend the entire time drinking yourself insensible at parties out of sheer depression. And that I think is a great curse. But from the point of view of an English diplomat the real curse is paper games because, as you know, the English have nothing whatsoever to say to each other but they're forced to entertain each other because it's sup-posed to promote morale. Actually, it used to drive my morale right down to rock bottom. You simply had to go; you couldn't refuse anybody senior to you—my head of chancery, my oriental counselor, my ambassador. As they didn't have much to say we used to sit and play "consequences" all evening with paper and pencil—these long long intellectual evenings became absolutely burnt into my memory. And even now I often awake screaming in the night playing a paper game with a British Dip.

The bad faith and secrecy have been very well done by Comp-ton McKenzie in his five books which analyse the situation in Athens during the first world war because in every country you have a divided optic on any given topic and it's amusing, exciting, and sometimes a tiny bit dangerous to try to find out exactly what's eating them and then convey that back. But our methods of spying nowadays are so ludicrous. Everything is really known technologically so that I should suppose that it won't be long now before, if you want to know what's going on in the Kremlin you could throw a switch somewhere in Pomona and listen to it. Which would be a great relief. A few jobs would be lost but in fact it would be a great relief because nothing very much is going on in the Kremlin that isn't going on just in this room. It's an attempt to bolster an idiocy, to blow it up as something important when it really isn't important at all. Nevertheless, one does have some exciting times. We had once an illustration which struck me as useful. There is one absolutely cardinal thing that the British are supreme masters of, and that is to say nothing and look idiotic. I'm not joking. Several times, just by not saying anything and not doing anything, people don't believe it's true. They come to you panicky with some bit of information such as the German's are 10 kilometers away, and you say, "Are they?" And it's clear that you wouldn't be in that complacent state if they were. So by not doing anything sometimes you can get away with murder. There is one particular example: in one of the most brilliant Italian feats during the war, three men in a baby submarine—commandos—came in and stuck plastic on the bottom of the biggest battleship we had at the moment in Alexandria harbour, the flagship of the Mediterranean fleet. In the middle of the night there was a dull explosion and the thing went down about 2 or 3 feet, but it stayed at anchor. As press attaché, they rang me up and said, "Do you know what's happened? We've caught these men but they've blown the whole bottom out of this ship." And of course these ships were surveyed all the time by the Germans by air making their calculations about the strength of the Mediterranean fleet in case of a fight at Oran or whatever. So it was really rather critical. They suggested that, "The best thing was to pretend that nothing has happened, old boy." It seemed to me quite a big pretend, but I said, "Okay, yes. We don't do anything." He said, "Absolutely nothing. Don't mention it." But though the explosion was very badly muffled the whole town felt it. It was like an earthquake. But it was muffled by the water and it was so deep down below, that, though the ship had subsided slightly and was absolutely out of action, it hadn't moved. So we just went around with what, in technical terms in my profession, is known as an operation poe-face—a chamberpot expression— for about five days. Strangely enough the event wasn't picked up by the press, nor by anybody, and that ship lay there for nearly five months before the enemy realised that it had the bottom blown completely out of if. A very useful thing, silence.

Also I had another ship experience that didn't endear the navy to me at all. I had one of those old rolltop desks, you know that kind you get in cheap offices everywhere downtown, and my secretary had got *Jane's Fighting Ships* and we got the entire Mediterranean fleet. We were trying to influence the French to give us a battleship and they wouldn't. We locked up all the machinery on their warships so they actually couldn't shoot at us, but they wouldn't go ashore and they wouldn't do anything. We didn't want to offend the Free French, you know, and so we were trying to get the French Admiral to come out on our side—trying to coerce a little bit. Then they said to me, "Can't you do some articles about the glories of the French fleet, and so on." So I had some articles like that and I put them in the rolltop desk. The next morning when I opened the desk to launch these articles they had disappeared. I said, "Oh, God, I've been burgled." They were all marked highly confidential. There was nothing that wasn't out of *Jane's Fighting Ships*, but still they were confidential. I had to report a confidential loss. Immediately the secret service visited me, the whole Scotland Yard came and took fingerprints and so on. I found other copies of the things and duly sent them out to the press, but this mystery was never cleared up until a month later when I opened the press and discovered that the roller had sucked the entire French fleet into the surround. But meanwhile everybody panicked. The French navy locked up their files and said that the Bulgarians were at it again. Moments of intense panic.

And in the middle of it another absurdity. I get a telegram from London saying, "George Bernard Shaw's film is being made by Mr. Pascal in Alexandria"—Anthony and Cleopatra, actually, a very bad film—"will you please look after the unit." It was the middle of the war, but I said yes, I would and got in touch with Mr. Pascal and arranged for barrels to put his film in to send it off. But he had perhaps 5,000 extras for battle scenes who were all Egyptians he picked up anywhere. He also had a false foam rubber Sphinx. Every day at the end of the shooting, they, the extras, didn't quite understand what was going on. They drew their salary and walked off with their costumes. The company was losing costumes at a rate of about 1,000 a day. At that time we had a bit of a fifth column phobia about parachutists. We had had such a bad mauling in Crete with the 1st division of the German parachutists being dropped. It was the first really extensive drop. Later the Army turned the tables on them at Arnhem. It was quite clear to us with our communications layout in the middle east and the internal sensibility of the Egyptians that perhaps a frightfully determined parachute drop might cut us off from the canal. It would be much worse havoc strategically than having to face Rommel nose to nose. So we were a bit sensitive to this element. At that time, in my office, I had an enormously spy-conscious man with popping eyes called Mr. Axelos who had a deep hoarse voice and smoked cigars, and he used to go about on a bicycle dressed in shorts with his beady eyes, all through the Arab quarter, looking for strange anomalies like, say, Italian parachutists disguised as nuns. And when he'd arrive at the office I'd say, "Mr. Axelos, how are things down at the airport?" And he'd say, *"C'est drole! C'est etrange! C'est trés etrange!"* Well, no sooner had Pascal begun to shoot there than Axelos began to go down more and more to the airport and he came back looking really purple. He said, "There's something really astonishing. I can't believe my eyes. It must be the Italian Air Force!" I said, "What's happened?" He said, "I've seen ancient Roman centurions walking about in the marketplace!" Of course it was these damned extras of Pascal's. They got so excited with their plumage they carried it off and used to do their evening shopping down there, which for a propagandist, was confusing to say the least. And then that foam rubber Sphinx caused terrible trouble, because the R.A.F. used the real one at Gizeh as a marker, to navigate by and they thought the Germans had dropped a dummy Sphinx to fool them.

These are some of the silly as well as interesting sides of diplomacy as it was yesterday. Perhaps things have changed, but I doubt it very much. Basically, I should say, Tallyrand's advice is really sound and can't be bettered. But the British contribution hasn't been negligible either. They have cultivated two secret weapons of great efficacy—the poe-face and the stiff upper lip. There's nothing like them when you are in a spot. Long may they flourish! }⊷—

*Designed & printed by Noel Young
for Capra Press in Santa Barbara,
February 1975. 250 numbered
copies, signed by the author,
were handbound by
Emily Paine.*